THE CHEMISTRY OF LIFE

A CBSE CLASS 10 STUDY GUIDE

AF577673

VIPUL BAIBHAV

Copyright © Vipul Baibhav
All Rights Reserved.

This book has been self-published with all reasonable efforts taken to make the material error-free by the author. No part of this book shall be used, reproduced in any manner whatsoever without written permission from the author, except in the case of brief quotations embodied in critical articles and reviews.

The Author of this book is solely responsible and liable for its content including but not limited to the views, representations, descriptions, statements, information, opinions and references ["Content"]. The Content of this book shall not constitute or be construed or deemed to reflect the opinion or expression of the Publisher or Editor. Neither the Publisher nor Editor endorse or approve the Content of this book or guarantee the reliability, accuracy or completeness of the Content published herein and do not make any representations or warranties of any kind, express or implied, including but not limited to the implied warranties of merchantability, fitness for a particular purpose. The Publisher and Editor shall not be liable whatsoever for any errors, omissions, whether such errors or omissions result from negligence, accident, or any other cause or claims for loss or damages of any kind, including without limitation, indirect or consequential loss or damage arising out of use, inability to use, or about the reliability, accuracy or sufficiency of the information contained in this book.

Made with ♥ on the Notion Press Platform
www.notionpress.com

This book is dedicated to all the students who are striving to achieve mastery in chemistry. It is our hope that this book will serve as a valuable resource for you as you navigate the challenging but rewarding world of chemistry. We would like to express our gratitude to all the educators who have dedicated their lives to teaching and inspire future scientists and chemist.

We would also like to thank our families for their love and support. Without their encouragement and understanding, this book would not have been possible.

Finally, we would like to express our appreciation to the CBSE board for providing a curriculum that challenges and inspires students to think critically and creatively.

Contents

Contents

Foreword

As a chemistry teacher and education expert, it is my pleasure to write the foreword for "The Chemistry of Life: A CBSE Class 10 Study Guide" written by Vipul Baibhav. This book is an essential resource for students who are preparing for their CBSE Class 10 chemistry exam, and I wholeheartedly recommend it to any student who wants to achieve mastery in chemistry.

The author, Vipul Baibhav, is an experienced educator and chemist with a passion for teaching. His ability to make complex chemical concepts easily understandable is evident in the clear and concise explanations provided in this book. The book covers all the topics included in the CBSE Class 10 chemistry curriculum, making it the perfect resource for students who want to achieve a high grade in their CBSE Class 10 chemistry exam.

The book also includes practice problems and exercises, designed to test students' understanding of the material and help them prepare for the CBSE Class 10 chemistry exam. This is an important feature as practice is crucial for students to master the subject.

In addition, the author's dedication to education and chemistry is evident in his work and he is highly respected by both his peers and students.

I highly recommend this book to all students who are preparing for their CBSE Class 10 chemistry exam and to any student who wants to deepen their understanding of the subject. It is an excellent resource that will help students achieve their goals and excel in chemistry.

Preface

It is with great pleasure that we present "The Chemistry of Life: A CBSE Class 10 Study Guide" to students preparing for their CBSE Class 10 chemistry exam. This book is the result of our collective effort to provide a comprehensive and easy-to-understand guide to the subject of chemistry.

Chemistry is a fascinating subject that plays an essential role in our daily lives, yet it can also be challenging for students to understand. That's why we have designed this book to be an accessible and engaging resource for students of all levels. The book covers all the topics included in the CBSE Class 10 chemistry curriculum, making it the perfect resource for students who want to achieve mastery in chemistry.

The book begins with an introduction to the fundamental concepts of chemistry, including chemical reactions and equations, acids, bases and salts, and metals and non-metals. It then delves into more advanced topics, such as carbon and its compounds, the periodic table and periodicity, and chemistry in everyday life.

Each chapter includes clear and concise explanations of key concepts, accompanied by diagrams and illustrations to help students understand difficult topics. The book also includes practice problems and exercises, designed to test students' understanding of the material and help them prepare for the CBSE Class 10 chemistry exam.

We believe that this book will serve as a valuable resource for students as they prepare for their CBSE Class 10 chemistry exam and as they continue to explore the world of chemistry. We hope that it will inspire students to develop a lifelong love of learning and a passion for the subject.

Acknowledgements

We would like to express our deepest gratitude to all the individuals and organizations that have helped us in creating "The Chemistry of Life: A CBSE Class 10 Study Guide."

First, we would like to thank our families and friends for their unwavering support and encouragement throughout the writing process. Without their love and understanding, this book would not have been possible.

We would also like to extend our appreciation to our colleagues and peers in the field of chemistry and education for their valuable feedback and suggestions. Their insights have greatly contributed to the quality of this book.

We are also grateful to the CBSE board for providing a curriculum that challenges and inspires students to think critically and creatively.

Finally, we would like to thank all the students who have used our book as a resource for their studies. Your feedback and support have been invaluable in helping us improve the book.

We hope that this book will serve as a valuable resource for students as they prepare for their CBSE Class 10 chemistry exam and as they continue to explore the world of chemistry.

Prologue

The study of chemistry is essential for understanding the world around us. From the air we breathe to the food we eat, chemistry plays a crucial role in our daily lives. It is the science that helps us understand the properties and behavior of matter, and how it changes through chemical reactions.

Chemistry is also a challenging subject, one that requires patience, perseverance and a willingness to think critically and creatively. The CBSE Class 10 chemistry curriculum is designed to introduce students to the fundamental concepts of chemistry and to develop their analytical and problem-solving skills.

This book, "The Chemistry of Life: A CBSE Class 10 Study Guide" is written with the intention to help students achieve mastery in chemistry and to excel in their CBSE Class 10 chemistry exam. It covers all the topics included in the CBSE Class 10 chemistry curriculum, providing clear and concise explanations of key concepts, accompanied by diagrams and illustrations to help students understand difficult topics.

The book also includes practice problems and exercises, designed to test students' understanding of the material and help them prepare for the CBSE Class 10 chemistry exam.

This book is not only for students preparing for their CBSE Class 10 chemistry exam but also for students who want to deepen their understanding of the subject and for those who want to develop a lifelong love of learning and a passion for chemistry.

We hope this book will serve as a valuable resource for students as they navigate the challenging but rewarding world of chemistry.

CHAPTER ONE

Introduction

Welcome to "The Chemistry of Life: A CBSE Class 10 Study Guide." This book is designed to help students achieve mastery in chemistry and excel in their CBSE Class 10 chemistry exam. Chemistry is an essential subject that helps us understand the properties and behavior of matter and how it changes through chemical reactions. It is the science that underlies the world around us and plays a crucial role in our daily lives.

The CBSE Class 10 chemistry curriculum is designed to introduce students to the fundamental concepts of chemistry and to develop their analytical and problem-solving skills. This book covers all the topics included in the CBSE Class 10 chemistry curriculum, providing clear and concise explanations of key concepts, accompanied by diagrams and illustrations to help students understand difficult topics.

The book is organized in a logical and easy-to-follow manner, making it easy for students to find the information they need. It includes practice problems and exercises, designed to test students' understanding of the material and help them prepare for the CBSE Class 10 chemistry exam.

In this book, you will learn about the basic concepts of chemistry such as atomic structure, chemical bonding, chemical reactions, states of matter, acids and bases, and more. You will also learn about the application of chemistry in everyday life, such as the chemistry of food, medicine, and the environment.

We understand that studying chemistry can be challenging, but with the help of this book, you will have all the tools you need to succeed. Our goal is to make the subject as clear and accessible as possible, so that you can develop a lifelong love of learning and a passion for chemistry.

We hope that this book will serve as a valuable resource for you as you prepare for your CBSE Class 10 chemistry exam and as you continue to explore the world of chemistry.

Overview of the chemistry curriculum for Class 10 CBSE

The CBSE Class 10 chemistry curriculum is designed to introduce students to the fundamental concepts of chemistry and to develop their analytical and problem-solving skills. The curriculum is divided into three sections:

- Chemical Substances - Nature and Behaviour: This section covers the basic concepts of chemistry such as atomic structure, chemical bonding, chemical reactions, states of matter, acids and bases, and more. It also covers the application of chemistry in everyday life, such as the chemistry of food, medicine, and the environment.
- World of Living: This section covers the chemistry of life, including topics such as the chemistry of biomolecules, metabolic reactions, and the chemistry of respiration and digestion.
- Effects of Chemical Substances on the Environment: This section covers the impact of chemical substances on the environment and the measures that can be taken to mitigate their negative effects. It includes topics such as air and water pollution, soil pollution, and the disposal of hazardous waste.

In addition to the above sections, the CBSE Class 10 chemistry curriculum also includes a section on practical work, which includes experiments and activities that are designed to help students develop their laboratory skills and apply the concepts they have learned in the classroom.

The curriculum also includes a section on project work, which encourages students to apply their knowledge of chemistry to real-world problems and to develop their research and critical thinking skills.

Overall, the CBSE Class 10 chemistry curriculum is designed to provide students with a solid foundation in the subject and to prepare them for further study in chemistry or related fields.

Importance of chemistry in everyday life

Chemistry plays an important role in everyday life, as it helps us understand the properties and behavior of matter and how it changes through chemical reactions. Some examples of the importance of chemistry in everyday life include:

1. Medicine: Chemistry plays a vital role in the development of new drugs and medical treatments. Medicines are developed using chemical compounds that interact with the body in specific ways to treat diseases.
2. Food: Chemistry is involved in the production, preservation, and preparation of food. It helps us understand the chemical reactions that occur during cooking and the preservation of food, and is also used to develop food additives and preservatives.
3. Environment: Chemistry helps us understand and address environmental issues, such as air and water pollution, soil contamination, and climate change. It is used to clean up hazardous waste and develop more environmentally friendly products.
4. Energy: Chemistry plays a crucial role in the production and use of energy. It helps us understand the chemical reactions that occur in fuels, such as gasoline and natural gas, and is used to develop alternative energy sources, such as solar and wind power.
5. Consumer products: Chemistry is involved in the development of a wide range of consumer products, including cosmetics, cleaning products, and personal care items. It helps us understand the properties of these products and how they interact with the human body.
6. Materials Science: Chemistry plays a vital role in developing new materials such as polymers, ceramics and composites.

Overall, chemistry is an essential subject that helps us understand the world around us and improves our quality of life in countless ways.

CHAPTER TWO

Chemical Reactions and Equations

Chemical reactions are the process by which atoms are rearranged to form new molecules. A chemical equation is a symbolic representation of a chemical reaction, which shows the reactants (starting materials) on the left side of the equation and the products (resulting materials) on the right side of the equation.

The chemical equation is written using chemical symbols and formulas to represent the reactants and products. The chemical symbols and formulas are usually written in a balanced form, which means that there is the same number of atoms of each element on both sides of the equation.

For example, the equation for the combustion of methane (CH4) is:

CH4 + 2O2 → CO2 + 2H2O

In this equation, CH4 represents methane, O2 represents oxygen, CO2 represents carbon dioxide, and H2O represents water. The equation is balanced because there are 1 carbon atom, 4 hydrogen atoms and 4 oxygen atoms on both sides.

Types of chemical reactions:

1. Combination reactions: In these reactions, two or more reactants combine to form a single product. The example above is a combination reaction.
2. Decomposition reactions: In these reactions, a single reactant breaks down into two or more products.
3. Displacement reactions: In these reactions, one element is replaced by another element in a compound.
4. Redox reactions: These reactions involve the transfer of electrons from one molecule to another.
5. Neutralization reactions: These reactions involve an acid and a base that neutralize each other to form a salt and water.
6. Precipitation reactions: These reactions involve two dissolved ionic compounds that react to form an insoluble solid, known as a precipitate.

Chemical reactions and equations are important concepts in chemistry because they help us understand how molecules interact and change, and how to predict the products of a reaction from the reactants. They also form the basis for many industrial processes, such as the production of fertilizers, medicines, and fuels.

Types of chemical reactions

There are several types of chemical reactions, including:

1. Synthesis reactions: two or more reactants combine to form a single product.
2. Decomposition reactions: a single reactant breaks down into two or more products.
3. Single replacement reactions: one element is replaced by another element in a compound.
4. Double replacement reactions: the ions of two compounds switch places to form two new compounds.
5. Combustion reactions: a substance reacts with oxygen to produce heat and light.
6. Acid-base reactions: an acid and a base react to form a salt and water.
7. Redox reactions: a chemical reaction in which there is a transfer of electrons from one molecule to another.
8. Hydrolysis reactions: chemical reactions in which water is used to break apart larger molecules into smaller ones.
9. Photochemical reactions: chemical reactions that are initiated by the absorption of light.
10. Biological reactions: chemical reactions that occur within living organisms.

Balancing chemical equations

Balancing chemical equations is the process of making sure that the number of atoms of each element is the same on both sides of the equation. This is important because the law of conservation of mass states that the total mass of the reactants must be equal to the total mass of the products. To balance a chemical equation, you can use the following steps:

1. Write the unbalanced equation, including the correct chemical formulas for all the reactants and products.
2. Count the number of atoms of each element on both sides of the equation.
3. Determine which side of the equation is not balanced and which element needs more atoms.
4. Place a coefficient (a number in front of a chemical formula) in front of the reactant or product that needs more atoms to balance the equation.
5. Check to make sure that the equation is now balanced, by counting the atoms of each element on both sides of the equation.
6. If the equation is not balanced, repeat steps 4 and 5 until the equation is balanced.

Example: Unbalanced equation: 2H2 + O2 -> 2H2O Balanced equation: 2H2 + O2 -> 2H2O

Note: You may need to adjust the coefficients multiple times until you get the balanced equation.

Redox reactions

Redox reactions, also known as oxidation-reduction reactions, involve a transfer of electrons from one molecule to another. These reactions are characterized by a change in oxidation state (oxidation number) of the atoms involved.

In a redox reaction, one species (the reducing agent) loses electrons while another species (the oxidizing agent) gains electrons. This can be represented by two half-reactions: the oxidation half-reaction and the reduction half-reaction. The oxidation half-reaction shows the loss of electrons by the reducing agent, and the reduction half-reaction shows the gain of electrons by the oxidizing agent.

To balance a redox reaction, the number of electrons lost must equal the number of electrons gained. This can be achieved by adjusting the coefficients in front of the chemical formulas in the half-reactions.

Example: The unbalanced redox reaction between zinc (Zn) and copper (II) ions in aqueous solution: Zn(s) + Cu2+(aq) -> Zn2+(aq) + Cu(s)

The oxidation half-reaction: Zn(s) -> Zn2+(aq) + 2e- The reduction half-reaction: Cu2+(aq) + 2e- -> Cu(s)

To balance the redox reaction, the number of electrons in the oxidation half-reaction must be equal to the number of electrons in the reduction half-reaction. We can balance the electrons by multiplying the number of electrons in the reduction half-reaction by 2: 2Zn(s) + Cu2+(aq) -> 2Zn2+(aq) + 2Cu(s)

Notice that in this example, zinc acts as a reducing agent and copper (II) ions act as an oxidizing agent.

Displacement reactions

Displacement reactions, also known as single replacement reactions, involve the replacement of one element by another element in a compound. This type of reaction occurs when a more reactive element displaces a less reactive element from a compound. The reactivity of elements can be determined by their position on the reactivity series.

In a displacement reaction, a metal element will displace another metal element from a compound, while a nonmetal element will displace another nonmetal element from a compound.

The general formula for a displacement reaction is:

A + BC -> AC + B

where A and B are elements, and BC is a compound containing element B.

Examples:

1. Zinc metal displacing copper ions from copper sulfate solution: Zn(s) + $CuSO_4$(aq) -> $ZnSO_4$(aq) + Cu(s)
2. Iron nails displacing hydrogen gas from hydrochloric acid: Fe(s) + HCl(aq) -> $FeCl_2$(aq) + H_2(g)
3. Chlorine gas displacing bromine from bromide ions: Cl_2(g) + 2Br^-(aq) -> 2Cl^-(aq) + Br_2(l)

It's important to note that not all elements will participate in displacement reactions, some elements are too unreactive to displace other elements from compounds. Additionally, some displacement reactions happen only under specific conditions, such as high temperature or pressure.

Practice problems and exercises

- Balancing Chemical Equations: Given a chemical equation, balance it according to the law of conservation of mass.

Example: $H_2 + O_2 \rightarrow H_2O$

Answer: $2H_2 + O_2 \rightarrow 2H_2O$

- Identifying Types of Reactions: Given a chemical equation, identify the type of reaction (synthesis, decomposition, single replacement, double replacement).

Example: $Fe + HCl \rightarrow FeCl_2 + H_2$

Answer: Single replacement reaction

- Predicting Products: Given the reactants, predict the products of a chemical reaction.

Example: $Na + Cl_2 \rightarrow$

Answer: NaCl

- Writing Chemical Equations: Given the reactants and products, write a balanced chemical equation.

Example: Magnesium metal reacts with hydrochloric acid to form magnesium chloride and hydrogen gas.

Answer: $Mg + 2HCl \rightarrow MgCl_2 + H_2$

- Combustion Reactions: Identify the reactants and products of combustion reactions.

Example: $C_2H_5OH + 3O_2 \rightarrow 2CO_2 + 3H_2O$

Answer: Reactants: Ethanol and Oxygen. Products: Carbon dioxide and water.

- Acids and Bases Reactions: Identify the reactants and products of reactions between acids and bases.

Example: $HCl + NaOH \rightarrow NaCl + H_2O$

Answer: Reactants: Hydrochloric acid and Sodium hydroxide. Products: Sodium chloride and water.

- Redox Reactions: Identify the oxidizing and reducing agents in a redox reaction.

Example: $MnO_2 + 4HCl \rightarrow MnCl_2 + Cl_2 + 2H_2O$

Answer: Oxidizing agent: MnO_2. Reducing agent: HCl.

CHAPTER THREE

Acids, Bases and Salts

Acids, Bases, and Salts are three important classes of chemical compounds that play a crucial role in a wide range of chemical reactions and processes.

Acids are compounds that release hydrogen ions (H^+) when dissolved in water. They have a sour taste and react with metals to produce hydrogen gas. Acids are typically represented by the formula HX, where X is a negative ion. Examples of common acids include hydrochloric acid (HCl), sulfuric acid (H_2SO_4), and citric acid ($C_6H_8O_7$).

Bases are compounds that release hydroxide ions (OH^-) when dissolved in water. They have a bitter taste and feel slippery to the touch. Bases are typically represented by the formula MOH, where M is a positive ion. Examples of common bases include sodium hydroxide (NaOH), calcium hydroxide ($Ca(OH)_2$), and ammonium hydroxide (NH_4OH).

Salts are compounds that are formed from the reaction of acids and bases. They are neutral compounds that do not release hydrogen ions or hydroxide ions when dissolved in water. Salts are typically represented by the formula MX, where M is a positive ion and X is a negative ion. Examples of common salts include sodium chloride (NaCl), potassium nitrate (KNO_3), and calcium sulfate ($CaSO_4$).

In chemical reactions, acids can react with bases to form salts and water. This reaction is known as neutralization. Neutralization reactions are important in many industrial and biological processes, including the production of fertilizers, the treatment of wastewater, and the regulation of acid-base balance in the human body.

In conclusion, Acids, Bases, and Salts play a crucial role in a wide range of chemical reactions and processes. Understanding the properties and behavior of these compounds is essential for students of chemistry and for anyone interested in the chemical sciences.

Acids and bases

Acids and bases are two important classes of chemical substances that are defined by their properties and behaviors.

An acid is a substance that, when dissolved in water, increases the concentration of hydrogen ions ($H+$) and has a sour taste. Acids have a pH value less than 7, meaning they are more acidic than neutral water. Some common examples of acids include hydrochloric acid (HCl), citric acid, and acetic acid.

A base, on the other hand, is a substance that, when dissolved in water, decreases the concentration of hydrogen ions and has a bitter taste. Bases have a pH value greater than 7, meaning they are more basic than neutral water. Some common examples of bases include sodium hydroxide ($NaOH$), potassium hydroxide (KOH), and calcium hydroxide ($Ca(OH)2$).

The relationship between acids and bases is described by the concept of pH, which measures the acidity or basicity of a solution on a scale of 0 to 14. Neutral substances have a pH of 7, while acidic substances have a pH less than 7 and basic substances have a pH greater than 7.

Neutralization reactions

Neutralization reactions are chemical reactions in which an acid reacts with a base to produce a salt and water. These reactions are characterized by the transfer of protons (H+) from the acid to the base. The transfer of protons results in the production of a neutral compound, hence the name "neutralization." The products of a neutralization reaction are typically a salt and water. The salt will have properties that depend on the properties of the original acid and base. For example, if the reaction involves a strong acid and a strong base, the salt produced will typically be soluble in water.

Neutralization reactions have important applications in many fields, including medicine, where they are used to neutralize harmful substances such as stomach acid. They are also used in the production of fertilizers, cleaning products, and many other industrial processes.

The balanced chemical equation for a neutralization reaction is typically written as:

$$\text{Acid} + \text{Base} \rightarrow \text{Salt} + \text{Water}$$

where the acid and base react in stoichiometric proportions to produce a salt and water.

The amount of acid and base required to produce a neutral solution depends on the relative strengths of the acid and base. Strong acids and bases typically react in a 1:1 ratio, while weaker acids and bases may require different ratios to achieve neutralization.

Salt preparation

Salt preparation refers to the process of synthesizing salts from acids and bases through a chemical reaction known as neutralization. Neutralization is a type of chemical reaction where an acid and a base react to form a salt and water.

The reaction between an acid and a base can be represented as follows:

Acid + Base -> Salt + Water

For example, when hydrochloric acid (HCl) reacts with sodium hydroxide (NaOH), the reaction produces sodium chloride (NaCl) and water:

$HCl + NaOH \rightarrow NaCl + H_2O$

The resulting salt depends on the type of acid and base used in the reaction. For example, when sulfuric acid (H_2SO_4) reacts with potassium hydroxide (KOH), potassium sulfate (K_2SO_4) is produced:

$H_2SO_4 + KOH \rightarrow K_2SO_4 + H_2O$

Salts are important in many industries and have a wide range of uses, including as food preservatives, in detergents and soaps, and in the production of fertilizers. To prepare a salt, the acid and base must be mixed in the correct proportion so that the reaction goes to completion and all of the acid is neutralized by the base. The resulting salt can then be separated from the water and collected.

pH and acid-base indicators

pH and acid-base indicators are important concepts in chemistry that relate to the strength of acids and bases.

pH stands for "potential of hydrogen" and is a measure of the concentration of hydrogen ions (H+) in a solution. A solution with a pH of 7 is considered neutral, meaning that the concentration of hydrogen ions is equal to the concentration of hydroxide ions (OH-). Solutions with a pH less than 7 are considered acidic, while solutions with a pH greater than 7 are considered basic or alkaline.

Acid-base indicators are substances that change color in response to changes in the pH of a solution. This allows us to quickly and easily determine the pH of a solution without using a pH meter. There are a variety of different acid-base indicators available, each with a different range of pH at which it changes color. For example, litmus paper is a common acid-base indicator that turns red in acidic solutions and blue in basic solutions.

In a neutralization reaction, an acid reacts with a base to produce a salt and water. The reaction helps to neutralize the pH of the solution, bringing it towards a pH of 7. For example, the reaction between hydrochloric acid (HCl) and sodium hydroxide (NaOH) produces sodium chloride (NaCl) and water:

$$HCl + NaOH \rightarrow NaCl + H2O$$

In this reaction, the hydrogen ions from the acid react with the hydroxide ions from the base to form water, while the remaining ions combine to form the salt. The result of this reaction is a neutral solution, as the concentration of hydrogen ions and hydroxide ions has been reduced.

By understanding the concepts of pH, acid-base indicators, and neutralization reactions, we can better understand the properties of acids, bases, and salts and how they react in different solutions.

Practice problems and exercises

Q1) What is an acid, and how can you identify an acidic solution using a pH indicator?

Ans: An acid is a substance that donates hydrogen ions (protons) in aqueous solution, producing a sour taste and releasing hydrogen gas. To identify an acidic solution, you can use a pH indicator. A pH indicator is a substance that changes color in response to changes in the hydrogen ion concentration (pH) of a solution. For example, litmus paper turns red in an acidic solution with a pH less than 7, while phenolphthalein changes from colorless to pink as the solution becomes more acidic. By observing the color change of the pH indicator, you can determine the acidic or basic nature of a solution.

Q2) What is a base, and how can you distinguish between a weak base and a strong base?

Ans: An acid is a substance that donates hydrogen ions (H+) in solution. Acids have a sour taste and can react with certain metals to produce hydrogen gas. The concentration of hydrogen ions in a solution is commonly expressed as the pH, which ranges from 0-14. A pH value less than 7 indicates an acidic solution, while a pH value greater than 7 indicates a basic or alkaline solution.

A base is a substance that accepts hydrogen ions (H+) in solution. Bases have a bitter taste and feel slippery to the touch. Bases can also neutralize acids, resulting in the formation of water and a salt. The strength of a base is related to its ability to accept hydrogen ions. A strong base has a high capacity for accepting hydrogen ions, while a weak base has a lower capacity.

To distinguish between a weak base and a strong base, you can use a pH indicator. The pH of a solution can indicate the strength of the base. A weak base will have a pH close to 7, while a strong base will have a pH greater than 7. Additionally, the amount of hydroxide ions (OH-) in a solution can also indicate the strength of the base. A solution with a higher concentration of hydroxide ions will be a stronger base than a solution with a lower concentration of hydroxide ions.

Q3)What is a salt, and how is it prepared by a neutralization reaction?

Ans: A salt is a chemical compound that is formed when an acid reacts with a base through a neutralization reaction. During a neutralization reaction, the hydrogen ions (H+) from the acid combine with the hydroxide ions (OH-) from the base to form water (H2O), and the remaining ions form the salt. The type of salt that is formed depends on the specific acid and base that react. For example, if hydrochloric acid (HCl) reacts with sodium hydroxide (NaOH), the salt that is formed is sodium chloride (NaCl). To prepare a salt, one must mix an appropriate amount of the acid and base together until the reaction reaches neutralization, which can be determined by using an acid-base indicator such as litmus paper or a pH meter.

Q5)What happens during a neutralization reaction between an acid and a base? How can you predict the products of a neutralization reaction?

Ans: A neutralization reaction is a chemical reaction between an acid and a base that results in the formation of a salt and water. During a neutralization reaction, the hydrogen ions from the acid react with the hydroxide ions from the base to form water. The remaining ions from the acid and base combine to form a salt.

To predict the products of a neutralization reaction, it is important to consider the type of acid and base being used. If the acid is a strong acid and the base is a strong base, the salt that forms will be neutral, meaning it will have a pH of 7. If the acid is a weak acid and the base is a strong base, the salt that forms will be basic, meaning it will have a pH greater than 7. If the acid is a strong acid and the base is a weak base, the salt that forms will be acidic, meaning it will have a pH less than 7.

Q6)How can you prepare a salt from an acid and a base, and what factors determine the properties of the salt formed?

Ans: In order to prepare a salt from an acid and a base, a neutralization reaction must take place. A neutralization reaction is a chemical reaction in which an acid and a base react to form a salt and water. During the reaction, the hydrogen ions (H+) from the acid combine with the hydroxide ions (OH-) from the base to form water, while the remaining ions from the acid and base combine to form the salt.

The properties of the salt formed during a neutralization reaction depend on several factors, including the type of acid and base used and the ratio of acid to base in the reaction. For example, if a strong acid reacts with a strong base, the salt produced will typically be neutral, while if a weak acid reacts with a strong base, the salt produced will be basic. Additionally, the cation and anion in the salt can also impact its properties, such as solubility and conductivity.

Q7)What is pH, and how can you use pH and acid-base indicators to determine the acidity or basicity of a solution?

Ans) In chemistry, pH is a scale used to measure the acidity or basicity of a solution. The pH scale ranges from 0 to 14, with 7 being neutral, less than 7 being acidic, and greater than 7 being basic or alkaline.

To determine the acidity or basicity of a solution, one can use pH and acid-base indicators. An acid-base indicator is a substance that changes color depending on the pH of the solution it is in. Some common examples of acid-base indicators include litmus paper and universal indicator solution.

For example, litmus paper turns red in an acidic solution and blue in a basic solution. Universal indicator solution, on the other hand, can show a range of colors from red (acidic) to yellow (neutral) to blue (basic) depending on the pH of the solution.

By using pH and acid-base indicators, a chemist can easily determine the acidity or basicity of a solution and make further predictions or conclusions about the solution's properties.

CHAPTER FOUR

Metals and Non-metals

Metals and Non-metals are two broad categories of elements that are distinguished based on their chemical and physical properties. Metals are known for their characteristic luster, high thermal and electrical conductivity, and malleability. They are usually solid at room temperature and are good conductors of heat and electricity. On the other hand, Non-metals are poor conductors of heat and electricity, are generally not malleable and are not lustrous. They are typically solids, liquids, or gases at room temperature and have properties that differ from metals. Some common examples of metals include copper, aluminum, iron, and gold. Common examples of non-metals include carbon, sulfur, nitrogen, and oxygen. The distinction between metals and non-metals is important in the fields of chemistry, materials science, and engineering.

Characteristics of metals and non-metals

Metals and non-metals are two distinct classes of elements that have different properties and characteristics. The properties of a metal or non-metal determine its behavior and the role it plays in the world around us.

Characteristics of Metals:

- Good conductors of heat and electricity
- Shiny and lustrous appearance
- Usually solid at room temperature
- Dense and have a high melting and boiling point
- Malleable and ductile, which means they can be easily shaped and stretched
- Generally found in the form of compounds in nature

Characteristics of Non-Metals:

- Poor conductors of heat and electricity
- Dull and non-lustrous appearance
- Usually a gas or a solid, but non-metals can also be in the liquid state
- Low density and have a low melting and boiling point
- Brittle, which means they break easily and cannot be shaped or stretched
- Often found in the elemental form or as compounds in nature.

These characteristics are important for understanding the behavior and reactivity of different elements and how they interact with each other in chemical reactions.

Chemical reactivity of metals and non-metals

Chemical reactivity refers to the ability of a substance to undergo chemical reactions and form new compounds.

Metals, in general, have high chemical reactivity and are known to react with non-metals to form compounds. Metals tend to lose electrons to form positive ions, or cations, which can bond with non-metal anions to form ionic compounds. Metals also tend to react with acids to produce hydrogen gas and a metal salt.

Non-metals, on the other hand, have low chemical reactivity. They tend to gain electrons to form negative ions, or anions, and do not easily react with other substances. However, some non-metals, such as halogens, are highly reactive and can readily form compounds with other elements.

The chemical reactivity of a metal or non-metal can also depend on its oxidation state, which determines its electron configuration and ability to react with other elements. For example, the reactivity of a metal can vary depending on whether it is in its elemental form or as an ion with a different oxidation state.

Extraction of metals

The extraction of metals refers to the process of obtaining pure metal elements from their ores. This process involves several steps such as mining the ore, crushing the ore, concentrating the ore, and then separating the metal from its impurities.

The first step in the extraction process is to mine the ore, which is the source of the metal element. The ore is then crushed into small pieces to make it easier to extract the metal. The next step is to concentrate the ore, which involves removing as many impurities as possible. This is usually done by using physical methods like flotation or magnetic separation.

Once the ore has been concentrated, it is then processed to separate the metal from its impurities. This step is known as the refining process, and it involves methods like electrolysis or distillation.

The choice of extraction method depends on various factors such as the type of metal, the availability of technology, and the cost involved. The extraction process for different metals is usually specific to the metal being extracted and is designed to achieve the maximum yield with the minimum amount of waste.

Practice problems and exercises

1. Classify the following elements as metals or non-metals based on their chemical and physical properties: sodium, chlorine, gold, oxygen, carbon, aluminum, nitrogen.
2. Write balanced chemical equations for the reactions between metals and non-metals with water or dilute acids.
3. Predict the type of reaction (oxidation, reduction, or displacement) that will occur between a metal and a non-metal in aqueous solution.
4. Explain the trend in reactivity of metals in terms of the electron configuration of their atoms.
5. Describe the process of extracting a metal from its ore, including the important steps and the chemicals used.
6. Discuss the environmental impact of metal extraction, including the release of pollutants and the depletion of natural resources.
7. Research a specific metal and its uses, including its properties and its role in modern technology and society.
8. Compare and contrast the properties of two different metals, including their reactivity, density, melting point, and other relevant characteristics.
9. Analyze the properties and reactivity of non-metals in terms of their electron configuration and the availability of electrons for chemical reactions.
10. Develop a visual representation or model of the periodic table that highlights the properties and reactivity of metals and non-metals.

CHAPTER FIVE

Carbon and its Compounds

Carbon is a chemical element with the symbol C and atomic number 6. It is one of the most important elements on Earth, as it forms the basis of all known life and is a major component of many organic and inorganic compounds. Carbon is unique in its ability to form strong covalent bonds with other carbon atoms, as well as with a variety of other elements, including hydrogen, oxygen, nitrogen, and sulfur. This versatility allows carbon to form an immense variety of compounds, ranging from simple sugars and fats to complex polymers and minerals. Carbon compounds play a vital role in many aspects of daily life, including energy production, medicine, and materials science.

Introduction to carbon compounds

Carbon compounds, also known as organic compounds, are a large and diverse group of compounds that contain the element carbon. They are essential for life on earth, and play a critical role in many biological processes, such as energy production and storage, as well as chemical communication. Carbon compounds are also the building blocks of important industrial and consumer products, such as fuels, plastics, and pharmaceuticals. The unique properties of carbon, such as its ability to form strong covalent bonds with other elements and its ability to form complex structures, make it a crucial component of these compounds.

Hydrocarbons

Hydrocarbons are a class of organic compounds composed entirely of hydrogen and carbon atoms. They are the building blocks of all organic molecules and play a crucial role in the energy industry as fuels and lubricants. There are three types of hydrocarbons: alkanes, alkenes, and alkynes. Alkanes are the simplest hydrocarbons, with only single bonds between the carbon atoms. Alkenes contain one or more double bonds between the carbon atoms, while alkynes contain one or more triple bonds between the carbon atoms. Hydrocarbons can be found in fossil fuels like coal, oil, and natural gas and can also be synthesized from renewable sources like plants and algae.

Organic chemistry

Organic chemistry is the study of the structure, properties, composition, reactions, and synthesis of organic compounds, which are compounds that contain carbon. Organic compounds form the basis of all living things and play a crucial role in the manufacture of many products, including food, fuels, plastics, and medicines. Organic chemistry also involves the study of reaction mechanisms, stereochemistry, and reactivity of organic molecules. The field of organic chemistry is broad and encompasses many sub-disciplines, including biochemistry, natural products chemistry, and synthetic chemistry.

Practice problems and exercises

1. Identify the functional groups in given organic compounds and explain their chemical reactivity.
2. Draw the structures of alkanes, alkenes, and alkynes and write their names.
3. Predict the products of reactions between different organic compounds, such as substitution reactions, elimination reactions, and addition reactions.
4. Balance chemical equations for reactions involving organic compounds.
5. Draw the structures of isomers of different organic compounds and explain their properties.
6. Predict the boiling and melting points of organic compounds based on their molecular structures.
7. Explain the formation and uses of different organic compounds, such as alcohols, carboxylic acids, esters, aldehydes, and ketones.
8. Describe the reaction mechanisms of different organic reactions, such as electrophilic aromatic substitution, nucleophilic substitution, and elimination reactions.
9. Predict the infrared spectra of different organic compounds and explain the functional group vibrations.
10. Explain the properties and uses of different polymers, such as nylon, polyethylene, and polystyrene.

CHAPTER SIX

Periodic Table and Periodicity

The periodic table is an essential tool for organizing and classifying the elements. It was first introduced by Dmitry Mendeleev in 1869 and has been continually refined over the years. The periodic table is arranged in order of increasing atomic number and is divided into rows (periods) and columns (groups or families).

Periodicity refers to the recurring patterns and trends in the properties of elements that are related to their position in the periodic table. Some of the properties that show periodicity include: electron configuration, atomic radius, ionization energy, electron affinity, and reactivity.

By studying the periodic table and the trends in properties of elements, scientists can make predictions about the properties of new elements and understand the behavior of elements in chemical reactions.

Elements and the periodic table

The periodic table is a graphical representation of all the known elements, organized in a way that allows for the prediction of the chemical and physical properties of elements based on their position in the table. The elements are arranged in rows and columns based on their atomic number, electron configuration, and chemical properties.

Each element in the periodic table is unique and has its own set of properties, including its atomic number, symbol, and name. The elements are grouped into families based on their chemical and physical properties, such as the alkali metals, alkaline earth metals, transition metals, non-metals, and noble gases. Understanding the arrangement and properties of elements in the periodic table is important for predicting chemical reactions and understanding the behavior of elements in different compounds.

Periodic properties

Periodic properties refer to the patterns and trends that exist among elements in the periodic table based on their atomic structure and electronic configuration. These properties include atomic size, ionization energy, electron affinity, electronegativity, and metal or non-metal characteristics. Understanding periodic properties allows us to make predictions about the reactivity and chemical behavior of elements and how they interact with other elements in chemical reactions.

Practice problems and exercises

1. What is the periodic table and why is it organized in a certain way?
2. What are the main elements found in the periodic table and what categories do they fall under (metals, non-metals, metalloids)?
3. What is meant by the term "periodicity" in reference to the periodic table?
4. How do the properties of elements change as you move across a period or down a group in the periodic table?
5. What are some examples of periodic properties and how can they be used to predict the behavior of elements in chemical reactions?
6. How does the electron configuration of an element influence its position in the periodic table and its properties?
7. How do the properties of the representative elements (s-block, p-block, d-block, and f-block) differ and what role do they play in chemical reactions?
8. How do the transition metals differ from the representative elements and what unique properties do they have?
9. How do the lanthanides and actinides differ from other elements in the periodic table and what unique properties do they have?
10. What is the significance of the periodic table in chemistry and how does it help predict the behavior of elements in chemical reactions?
11. What is the periodic table and why is it organized in a certain way?
12. What are the main elements found in the periodic table and what categories do they fall under (metals, non-metals, metalloids)?
13. What is meant by the term "periodicity" in reference to the periodic table?
14. How do the properties of elements change as you move across a period or down a group in the periodic table?
15. What are some examples of periodic properties and how can they be used to predict the behavior of elements in chemical reactions?
16. How does the electron configuration of an element influence its position in the periodic table and its properties?
17. How do the properties of the representative elements (s-block, p-block, d-block, and f-block) differ and what role do they play in chemical reactions?
18. How do the transition metals differ from the representative elements and what unique properties do they have?
19. How do the lanthanides and actinides differ from other elements in the periodic table and what unique properties do they have?
20. What is the significance of the periodic table in chemistry and how does it help predict the behavior of elements in chemical reactions?

CHAPTER SEVEN

Chemistry in Everyday Life

Chemistry is a branch of science that studies the composition, properties, and reactions of matter. Chemistry plays a crucial role in our daily lives and has a significant impact on various aspects of modern society. From the food we eat to the medicine we take, chemistry is present in every aspect of our daily lives. Understanding the principles of chemistry can help us make informed decisions and understand the science behind many of the things we use and consume every day.

Chemistry in medicine

Chemistry plays a crucial role in the development and production of medicines. From the synthesis of active pharmaceutical ingredients to the formulation of drugs, chemistry is involved in every step. Understanding the chemical properties of medicines helps in their proper storage, transportation, and administration. Additionally, understanding the chemical reactions between drugs and the body can help in predicting their therapeutic effects and potential side effects. Furthermore, advances in chemical research have led to the development of new drugs, diagnostic tools, and treatments, making chemistry an essential part of modern medicine.

Chemistry in industry

Chemistry plays a crucial role in many industries, including:

- Pharmaceuticals: Developing and producing medicines and drugs
- Materials Science: Developing new materials with specific properties
- Energy: Developing fuels and alternative energy sources
- Consumer Goods: Developing and producing personal care and household products
- Agriculture: Developing and producing fertilizers, pesticides and herbicides
- Food and Beverage: Developing and producing food additives, preservatives and packaging materials
- Environmental: Developing solutions for environmental issues such as pollution control.

Chemists in these industries use their knowledge of chemical reactions and properties to create new products, improve existing ones, and ensure their safety and efficacy.

Environmental chemistry

Environmental Chemistry is the study of the behavior, fate, and effects of chemicals in the environment. It involves the use of chemical principles and techniques to understand the interactions of chemicals with the environment and living organisms.

Applications of Environmental Chemistry include:

- Water Quality: Monitoring and controlling contaminants in water resources
- Air Quality: Studying and reducing air pollution from industrial and vehicular sources.
- Soil Contamination: Identifying and remediating contaminated soils
- Climate Change: Understanding the impact of human activities on the Earth's climate and developing solutions.
- Hazardous Waste Management: Developing safe methods for disposal and treatment of hazardous waste.
- Sustainable Chemistry: Developing and promoting environmentally friendly chemical processes and products.

Environmental Chemists work to understand the impact of chemicals on the environment and human health, and to develop strategies to minimize or prevent those impacts.

Practice problems and exercises

Q1)Identify the chemical reactions taking place in the following everyday situations:

a. Cooking an egg b. Baking bread c. Rusting of iron

Q2)Explain how soap works to remove grease and dirt from clothes. What is the chemical reaction that occurs?

Q3)Discuss the importance of pH in our daily lives. Provide examples of how pH affects our health and the environment.

Q4)Discuss the role of enzymes in our digestive system and how they help to break down food.

Q5)Explain the chemical reactions taking place during photosynthesis in plants. How does this process provide the energy for almost all living organisms on Earth?

Q6)Discuss the impact of acid rain on the environment. What is the chemical reaction that causes acid rain, and how can it be prevented?

Q7)What are polymers and how are they used in everyday life? Provide examples of common polymers and their uses.

Q8)Explain the difference between physical and chemical changes and provide examples of each.

Q9)Discuss the importance of water quality and the role of water treatment in ensuring safe drinking water. What are the common methods used to purify water, and how do they work?

Q10)What is the chemical reaction that occurs when you light a match? How does this reaction release energy in the form of heat and light?

CHAPTER EIGHT

Conclusion

As the author of The Chemistry of Life: A Guide to CBSE Class 10 Chemistry, I would like to express my sincere gratitude to the readers for joining me on this journey to explore the wonders of chemistry. I hope that this book has provided a comprehensive and engaging introduction to the subject and has sparked an interest in the readers to learn more about the chemistry of life.

Throughout the book, we have covered a wide range of topics, including chemical reactions, acids and bases, organic chemistry, biochemistry, and environmental chemistry, among others. We have also explored the practical applications of chemistry in our daily lives and its impact on the world around us.

In conclusion, I would like to emphasize the importance of chemistry in our lives and the crucial role it plays in shaping the future. Chemistry has the power to unlock new discoveries, solve complex problems, and improve the quality of life for all. It is my hope that the readers will continue to cultivate their curiosity about chemistry and use the knowledge and skills gained from this book to make a positive impact on the world.

Thank you again for reading The Chemistry of Life: A Guide to CBSE Class 10 Chemistry, and I wish you all the best in your future studies and endeavors.

Printed by Libri Plureos GmbH in Hamburg,
Germany